"Any membership business knows the importance of monthly recurring revenue. However, most struggle to increase their MRR month over month. Just follow Scott's simple advice and you'll accelerate your recurring revenue, get more members, and have a solid membership business."

—SHAUN BUCK, Founder, www.NewsletterPro.com

"*Accelerate* is a must read for any membership or association leader. Scott Whitaker knows his stuff. Together we built a membership that became the largest membership organization in its niche. Accelerator #8 is one that we use to this day to get more members. If you're looking to rapidly grow your membership or you're looking for proven methods and tools to help you break your barriers to growth, then *Accelerate* is a must read!"

—NELSON SEARCY, Founder, www.RenegadePastors.com

"Thank you, Scott, for putting this into a simple process that will increase our revenue and more importantly our client loyalty."

—JENNIFER SANCHEZ, VP of Sales & Marketing
Beautique Medical Spa

"Since following Scott guidance, I have increased my income by 50% per month. I've also been able to provide better service, increase member engagement, and have higher retention rates."

—JEANNETTE KOCZELA, Founder/President
Int'l Association of Professional Life Coaches®

"Scott Whitaker is a membership master! Two tips in under five minutes helped double our monthly membership revenue. Double! No bull."

—TODD TRAMONTE, Real Estate Coach

ACCELERATE

How to Get Your Next 10, 100,

500, or Even 1,000 Members

...And Why Most Memberships,

Associations and Coaches Never Do!

SCOTT WHITAKER

Foreword by Kim Walsh Phillips

Year of the Book

135 Glen Avenue

Glen Rock, PA 17327

Print ISBN: 978-1-949150-84-1

The information provided in this book is for general informational purposes only. This is not a "get rich quick" scheme. It is about building a solid business that serves and brings value to clients. Any and all claims or representations, as to income earnings, are not to be considered as average earnings. There can be no assurance that any prior successes, or past results, as to income earnings, can be used as an indication of your future success or results. As with any business endeavor, you assume all risk related to investment and money based on your own discretion and at your own potential expense. Always seek the advice of a professional when making financial, tax, or business decisions.

To my wife Kelly and our two beautiful daughters,
Mackenzie and Emily.

ACKNOWLEDGMENTS

This is the first of many books to come. None would be possible without my wife, best friend, and biggest fan, Kelly. We've taken some enormous steps of faith that I would have never been able to do on my own, nor would I want to with anyone else. Your support has helped make all this possible.

To Mackenzie and Emily, you've taught me so much about life, love, and being a dad. I've carried many titles in this world, but being your dad is one of the greatest of all.

I'm extremely grateful to Mike Agugliaro, who brought out the "Dark Warrior" and nudged me back to the "relentless" pursuit to help others, build a high impact business, and never settle for less. Thanks for the privilege to play a small role in helping build your movement.

A very special thanks to my friend Kim Walsh Phillips who has been a constant encouragement and has helped propel my voice and locate my "super power." I'm grateful for your friendship and the many ways you have helped me to help others.

I'm eternally grateful to my friend Nelson Searcy. Together we got to experience the grand adventure of launching a membership business and building it from the ground up. You taught me discipline, generosity, how to manage others, systems, and so much more that has helped me succeed in life. I am eternally grateful for the impact you allowed me to share in.

A special thanks to Demi Stevens for edits, design, and guidance through this publishing process. Thanks for giving these words life and just making it all sound good. HA!

Finally, I'm grateful to my God who has brought me on this journey of faith. Much of what I've learned has come from being a member of what I consider to be the oldest membership of all-time – the local Church. And to not only be a member but the privilege of being able to pastor a congregation. To all my Pastor friends, know that you are leading the greatest membership organization in all the world. There is no other membership that has the eternal impact you're having.

TABLE OF CONTENTS

FOREWORD

Back when I had my marketing agency, I rarely took a vacation.

If I wasn't working, I wasn't making money because I was paid by the hour... a fee for service. The hourly rate was great, but with the expenses of running a company, it still required me to work all the time just to make ends meet.

Plus, to be frank, there was a little voice inside of me (I call it God, you can call it what you like), telling me I was meant to reach more people all along.

Eventually, while reading a newsletter for a membership program I belonged to, I got an idea... what if I created a newsletter that could be offered to others for a subscription fee? That way my clients could receive content from me and I could afford to mail it because the actual subscribers would cover its cost.

Now, that program has grown into the Powerful Professionals Business Coaching. Of course, it is more robust with monthly Masterclasses, a vibrant Facebook Group community, live events and more... but we started simple. Without that beginning we wouldn't have the community we have now.

And that would be even more tragic than Adam Levin's performance at the 2019 Super Bowl.

Today it is so much easier than ever to start your membership program. With resources like Facebook Groups and video meeting software, you can literally launch for free.

In case you are thinking this just has to be all business... it doesn't. Your membership program can be based on a topic you simply find interesting.

Whether for building your core business or a side passion, having a membership program gives you a way to reach more people than you ever could one-on-one. It also leverages your time because you can create a piece of content once and it can serve all of your members.

(A virtual photocopy machine for your fabulous self.)

Many of my tribe members have their own membership programs... in all sorts of niches.

Cathy Frost has one for her "Never Diet Again" program.

Mastermind member Jennifer Sanchez created one for her Med Spa clients.

Powerful Professionals Business Coaching member David Stetzel has one for his Cyber Security focused niche and Valerie Hart built one for those who want to communicate better with their pets.

Mastermind member Todd Tramonte created one for other realtors and Tristan and Sabrina Truscott have one for Dojos and healers.

Some are business. Some are not. All are incredible in that they are changing lives and leveraging time.

Through membership programs, we can create content once, yet earn revenue over and over again. Plus, we are able to serve a lot more people in this platform than we ever could if we tried to assist everyone one-on-one.

I've worked with Scott Whitaker on my membership program for the past year. He's helped not only with its vision, but also its scale and growth. Plus, he helped me launch two Mastermind programs in the past year... one of my favorite things ever in my career.

And one of his greatest super powers? Retention and growth in the most profitable way possible. He's a genius when it comes to member engagement and ensuring that when they stay, they pay.

(I'm without a cocktail while writing this, so I won't go into the painful details, but let's just say I didn't have it together on making sure members were paying before working with Scott.)

I've also been a witness to Scott's magic for other membership businesses of my colleagues – helping them launch new membership levels, create masterminds, and increase member retention. Many of their examples fill this book's pages you are about to read. Each is a treasure you can use in your own membership business.

Gratitude to Scott for writing this book at my request after the frustration of finding nothing like it on the market.

To you, reader... Enjoy. You are about to embark on an incredible journey of multiplying your membership.

—Kim Walsh Phillips
Powerfulprofessionals.com

YOU CAN CREATE IMMEDIATE RECURRING REVENUE

(IT IS POSSIBLE!)

It started in a hotel lobby in Orange County, California. My first membership business hit a plateau. We grew the membership from 72 members to 354 and we were stuck.

Many would have been satisfied with having 354 members. But when you lead a membership business – one that you know is going to make an impact, change people's lives, create better relationships, improve their finances, and help them live a healthier life – then you know you can't just stop at any plateau. You're on a mission to help as many people as possible.

To break through, we tried all sorts of marketing, hired experts, and ran a number of campaigns, but we just weren't growing. Sure, we would add members, but then we would lose members, too. The number of new members just couldn't outpace the churn of those canceling.

Which takes us back to that hotel lobby in Orange County, CA. My colleague and founder of the business, Nelson Searcy, and I were set to meet. I laid out the plan to create a new membership – one that would finally break the barrier we were facing, enabling us to help more people and ultimately fulfill the mission that we were set upon.

After I laid out the plan, it was then and there that we first believed, "It *is* possible!"

Whoever said, "I never thought it was possible," lied.

Your belief that a goal CAN be accomplished always comes BEFORE making the goal happen.

You must believe that something can be, before it will become.

If you currently have a membership business and are looking to add more members, expand your impact, and move from just adding members to multiplying your membership – it is possible.

If you're thinking about starting a membership from scratch, taking what you know and helping other people achieve their goals, starting with very little or even no money at all – it is possible.

Within two weeks of leaving that hotel lobby, we began to sell the new membership level. And two weeks after that, we went from adding members to literally multiplying our membership. We sold well over 100 memberships in the very first month alone.

Six months later, our membership had grown from 354 members to over 700 members. Our recurring revenue multiplied, and we were suddenly a multi-million dollar membership business.

Recurring revenue is the company revenue that is predictable and more likely to continue into the future. It's not a one-time purchase, but rather a commitment on behalf of the member to continue to pay for the goods and services your company provides.

It's a mutual commitment. When you make a commitment to provide your valuable content and services, your members make a commitment to pay for that membership on a recurring basis.

We continued to multiply our new members and revenue, ultimately growing to over 3,127 total memberships.

That's when I set out on a new mission... a mission to help others do the same. Helping others multiply their mission, impact, and membership. Since then, I've been able to repeat this multiplication effect in numerous other membership businesses.

- Mike Agugliaro, Founder of CEO Warrior, sold over a million dollars in membership in 21 days.

- Kim Walsh Phillips, Founder of Powerful Professionals, sold over $240,000 in membership in less than 30 days.

- Kris Murray, Founder of Childcare Marketing, sold over $460,000 in membership in less than six months.

- Michael Rozbruch, Founder of Roz Strategies, sold well into six figures of membership in less than four months and increased retention on current membership.

And there are others: Tom Orent, Jeannette Kozcela, Val Heart, Steve Anderson, Lisa Phillips; all of them have built six- and seven-figure membership businesses. Some of them did so from scratch.

What you're going to discover in the following pages are the repeatable "accelerators" that make monthly recurring revenue possible. These accelerators will help you launch a new membership, multiply your current membership, raise the value of what you're currently providing to your members, and uncover new opportunities that already exist in your membership.

Whether you're an association with thousands of members, looking for thousands more; a membership looking to add tens and hundreds of members; a coach looking for dozens of members; there's one thing we all have in common – *we're in the business of membership!*

Regardless of what you provide, how you provide it, or when you provide it, there are a number of commonalities across all of our niches – we've set out to provide a membership and it is funded on recurring revenue (whether it be annual or monthly).

Recurring revenue is where it's at!

It's the lifeblood of our business. It makes everything happen. It enables us to multiply our membership, hire staff, provide more services, and give greater value.

Most of all, it funds the mission of your membership. Recurring revenue for some may be the end result, but for me and the membership businesses I work with, it is the means to an end of making a greater impact on the lives of our members.

If you're ready to multiply your membership and money, believe it is possible!

"Your guidance and coaching there was invaluable. I'm proof positive that a membership program has real, calculable, closing-table value that goes far beyond the empty echoes of "...a really good reputation." Memberships are worth money today, every month thereafter, and then they multiply again when you go to sell your business... In my case the value created was well into 7 figures. Thank you for your continued guidance."

—ADAMS HUDSON
President, HudsonInk.com

TAKE A MEMBER FROM 'SIGN-UP' TO 'FULLY ENGAGED'

I signed up for a gym one time. Yeah! That's right, it was just one time. I'm a pretty healthy guy. I try to watch what I eat but I've never really been the one to go to the gym on a regularly scheduled regimen. But it was the New Year and I figured why not give it a try.

However, after signing up, my travel calendar quickly filled and I never made it to the gym.

I even had a friend who went to the same gym. He invited me to come and work out, but I just never made it a priority to go.

Then I figured I'd make it a game. Not some game where I'm going to go and sweat until I can't sweat any more, or some game where you workout until the point of breaking a bone.

For me it became a "membership game." I began to wonder, "How long will it take the gym to contact me and actually get me to use my membership?"

Being in the membership business, I'm constantly watching what other membership businesses are doing. I watch how they build their membership, what they do to increase engagement and beat their churn rate.

Now it was a matter of waiting... waiting to see how long I could go before they asked me to fully engage in my membership.

57 days! It took them 57 days to get me to take some sort of action to use my membership.

I found out from a friend who went to the same gym that he talked to the owner and said, "You really ought to call Scott and get him in here. You know he's a membership expert."

I then received a phone call from the gym inviting me to come and workout and take an assessment. They scheduled an appointment so I went in.

Did it work? No!

I showed up for my assessment only to be put through a sales process where they attempted to upsell me on personal training.

You can imagine the look on the sales guy's face when I told him that two personal training sessions were already included with my membership and I wasn't about to purchase more.

If there's anyone who doesn't mind being upsold it's me. I appreciate a good salesperson, working their craft and seeking to help more people. Every time someone signs up for membership, they do just that! They sign up. To you and me, that may sound like they've become a member. But in that person's mind, they only just signed up. They simply made a transaction.

If you asked the owner of the gym, "Is Scott a member?" the owner would have said, "Yes! He's all paid up. He's a member!"

But if you asked me, "Are you a member of [blank] Gym?" I would have said, "No! I signed up, but I never go."

Most membership businesses have an intentional sales process, just like the gym I signed up for. But most membership businesses never have an intentional process by which they move a member from signing up to becoming fully engaged in the membership.

By the way, a year after I signed up for the gym, they closed their doors. They went out of business. And without a doubt in my mind, one of the reasons they did so is because they were not intentionally getting people engaged in their membership.

You need more than an intentional sales process... you need to intentionally engage customers to grow into a feeling of MEMBERSHIP.

Before you acquire a member, you really need to know what you're going to do with every new person who signs up. I call this the "Assimilation Accelerator."

When you assimilate people into your membership, they go from saying, "I signed up," to saying, "I'm a member of..."

And there's a simple step-by-step process to make this happen.

It looks like this:

WHAT DO YOU WANT YOUR MEMBERS TO RECEIVE:

- In the first HOUR

- In the first DAY

- In the first WEEK

- In the first MONTH

Let's break it down:

WHAT DO YOU WANT YOUR MEMBERS TO RECEIVE IN THE **FIRST HOUR?**

Imagine for a moment, you just bought a car. You spent time deciding which make and model you wanted to buy. You may have considered leasing versus buying and tried to decide which was best for your budget.

Then, you spent time checking out dealerships trying to find a reputable dealer. You may have even asked some friends about their recent experiences.

Next, you went and started test-driving your future commuting machine. You tested the comfort, you turned the knobs, pushed the buttons. If you're like me, you even looked under the hood pretending to know what you're actually looking at.

And then finally, it happened. You made a decision. You decided this is the car for you. You told the salesperson (after a little haggling) to get the papers together and "let's sign."

The salesperson lined everything up for you. You signed and then they took you to the side entrance of the dealership. And there it is!

They present you with your new car! It has the red carpet rolled out for you. The doors are open, the car has obviously been washed, waxed, and fully detailed inside and out.

They hand you the keys, shake your hand, and congratulate you as the new owner.

You get the picture. You put down the money and they made a presentation all within the first hour.

WHEN IT COMES TO MEMBERSHIP, WHAT ARE YOU DOING?

How are you rolling out the red carpet for your brand-new member?

They just gave you the money. What are you giving them in return?

For many membership businesses, it's a receipt and that's it. For others, they may get a receipt and some automated email.

In the first hour of membership, how are you moving people from saying, "I just signed up," to making them feel like, "I'm actually a member."

What can you give your new member to make them feel different? To make them see that members are treated differently?

Let's face it. It can be tough to "present your membership" to someone. After all, they're buying a membership. How do you transform that transaction and make it into an experience?

There are a number of ways that I've coached businesses on how to do this. You can get a free action guide on how to move your membership from a transaction to an experience. Just go to: www.AcceleratorBook.com.

WHAT DO YOU WANT YOUR MEMBERS TO RECEIVE IN THE **FIRST DAY?**

Let's go back to our story. You take your new car home. Instead of parking it in the garage, you decide to park it in the driveway. Call it arrogance, call it excitement, either way, you park in the driveway so you can show it off.

Plus, every now and then you like to peek out the window and say to yourself, "Now that's a good looking car right there!"

You wake up the next day, and you're off to work. Your commute seems different. Maybe it's because you no longer feel the potholes that line the highway. There's a better handling of the turns. The sound system is crisp. The windows are tight and you no longer hear the air seeping in. It's just a great experience.

You go through your workday and then around lunch time you get a phone call. The Caller ID shows that it's the dealership. Your heart skips a beat. You immediately think, "Maybe something went wrong with the paperwork." "Maybe there was some sort of mistake."

You answer the phone and the person on the other end says he's the General Manager of the dealership. He says to you, "Hey, this is John Doe, from 'The Best Ever Dealership' and I was just calling to see how you're enjoying your new vehicle. I was just calling to see if you had any questions and to make sure that everything is going well."

You respond and let him know that you're enjoying your car. You may even ask a question or two about how to operate the new climate control system or what those buttons under the rearview mirror do.

He answers your questions, congratulates you again on your purchase, and thanks you for choosing "Best Dealership Ever."

You hang up the phone and you have a sense of pride. Pride in knowing you chose the right dealership. Pride in knowing you have someone who actually cared enough to call you after the purchase, just to make sure you have what you need.

When It Comes to Your Membership, What Are You Doing Within the FIRST DAY?

By providing something for your member within the first day, you're affirming the decision they already made. There's no buyer's remorse.

You give your member the confidence they need. The confidence in knowing they made a right decision.

They begin to "experience their membership" on a new level. You're humanizing the transaction that took place on the previous day, showing that you really do care for your members and that they're not just some name on a database.

Most often, I encourage membership businesses to make it a phone call. In our digital age, a phone call goes a long way.

It doesn't have to be a long conversation. As a matter of fact, it's best to keep it short. Have a script to follow. Don't try to answer all of your new member's questions. You don't have to be prepared for that. Just give them the confidence that you'll get them the answer if you don't know.

Imagine if the General Manager received a question about how to increase the horsepower of the new car by increasing the air intake and if that was something that could be customized to your new vehicle.

Remember: You don't have to know all the answers... just give them the assurance that you'll get them an answer to their question.

Do you think he would know the answer? Of course not! He'd probably say, "That's a great question! Let me have my Service Manager contact you and see what we can do to increase the horsepower even more. Is tomorrow between 3pm and 5pm a good time to reach you?"

You don't have to have all the answers, just give them the assurance that you'll get them an answer to their question. The goal is to create a welcoming experience the day after they sign up for your membership.

You can get a free "Welcome Call Script" to tweak and make your own. Just go to: www.AcceleratorBook.com.

WHAT DO YOU WANT YOUR MEMBERS TO RECEIVE IN THE **FIRST WEEK?**

Back to our story. The new car smell is still there. Your friends, neighbors, and family members are starting to ask questions. Maybe they're going to be in the market for a new car soon, too.

By now, there's no going back. You love your new purchase. It's a week later and you get home from work and there's a FedEx package on your doorstep.

It has a big yellow sticker that says, "Overnight Delivery." You know it's important if they sent it overnight. You go inside and you take another look at the label. You see that it's from the "Best Dealership Ever."

Now you're really curious. What's inside? Surely, it's not your license plate. The DMV takes up to 30 days just to make that happen. It would be nice, but you know it's not that.

You open the package and there's a lovely presentation guide with the contact information of the dealership. There's a really nice collector's guide that is all about your brand new car. And on top of that, there's a thank you gift. It's a gift card to the "The Best Ever Restaurant" in town.

The handwritten note that came with the gift card reads:

> Hey John,
>
> Thanks again for choosing "The Best Ever Dealership." Enclosed are a couple of gifts. It's just our way of saying thanks for allowing us to assist you in choosing the car you desired.
>
> If there's any way we can help you or someone you know in the future, don't hesitate to let us know.
>
> Thanks again!

You think to yourself, "I would have never expected to receive this. Wow! Not only do I have a great car, I'm getting a date night out!"

It is evident that the dealership has gone out of their way to make sure their customers have the best possible experience.

WHEN IT COMES TO YOUR MEMBERSHIP, WHAT ARE YOU DOING WITHIN THE FIRST WEEK?

What can you provide your members that will make them say, "Wow!?"

Depending on your membership, it can be big or small. Different memberships have different fees and levels of investment.

For some, it may be just a handwritten note. For others, it may be a gift card. And for others it may be a nice designed package that is delivered overnight.

Again, the goal isn't how much you spend on the "wow gift." Instead, it is how well you communicate that the new member is more than a customer – they're a member. They now belong in your community.

What makes something a "Wow gift"?

- It's unexpected
- It's personalized
- It's presented in an attention getting manner
- It's desirable
- It has value
- It makes the recipient want to tell others

If you can hit all of these points, you'll have a "wow" gift for your new members and one that will get them talking about "their membership."

You'll hear them tell their friends, "I'm a new member of this 'Best Ever Membership' and you'll never guess what they did…"

No longer will they say, "I signed up for…" But instead they'll now say, "I'm a member of…"

WHAT DO YOU WANT YOUR MEMBERS TO RECEIVE IN THE **FIRST MONTH?**

Let's conclude our story with "The Best Ever Dealership." It's been a month now. Your purchase is starting to lose that new car smell. It's starting to smell more like a "daily driver." Maybe it's the sweat from having sat in rush hour traffic or the spilled ketchup from that lunch (even though you swore you would never eat in your brand-new car).

Either way, the car is starting to feel like it's yours. You've found the right adjustments for your seat and mirrors. Your Bluetooth is connected, and everything is now personalized.

There's just one thing missing.

Your license plate has yet to arrive. There's just five more days remaining on your 30-day temporary license. The DMV is taking their time and you're left waiting on the mail.

At long last, your license plate arrives. You get to finally take the temporary tag down and put the real license plate on.

Just when you put the screwdriver away, your spouse comes in and hands you a big envelope. You notice the return address, "The Best Dealership Ever."

You think to yourself, "I should be surprised, but they've taken such great care of me."

You open the big envelope and inside is a nice letter from your salesman along with a gift certificate for a free oil change and tire rotation.

"They've really outdone themselves this time." Now you're a diehard fan and the next time you're in the market for a car, you know where you're going.

WHEN IT COMES TO YOUR MEMBERSHIP, WHAT ARE YOU DOING WITHIN THE FIRST MONTH?

Are you creating a membership experience that motivates your new members to create anticipation of what's next?

Are you helping your members utilize what your membership promises to deliver?

Have you actually shown your members how to use their membership?

Most membership businesses are leaving their membership to chance. What does that mean? Your members might use it, or they might not. You're not really sure if they're actually doing what you desire for them to do with the membership.

The goal is to create a welcoming experience long after the sign-up occurs and assimilate them into a member.

For free sample emails, letters, gifts and tools to help you assimilate your new members, visit:

www.AcceleratorBook.com

THEY'RE MEMBERS – BUILD YOUR MEMBERSHIP INTO COMMUNITY

What most separates a membership business from a "customer-based" business?

The list is rather long:

- MRR (Monthly Recurring Revenue)
- Retention
- Churn
- Trial membership
- Membership pathway
- Assimilation
- Upgrades
- Downgrades
- Content calendar (when you're going to provide what you provide)
- Cancelations
- Reactivations
- "Members Only" events, services, products
- Community

In my opinion, it's that last point that most separates members from customers – COMMUNITY.

I have yet to see a membership where there isn't a community.

[Note: I make a distinction between subscriptions and memberships. No one says, "I'm a member of Netflix." Or, "I'm a member of the *Wall Street Journal*." That's because those are clearly subscriptions. Subscriptions would be better served if they created a community. However, I'll leave that topic for another book.]

Community is the greatest tool a membership business has. It is unique to every membership. It cannot be duplicated or copied.

What makes a "customer" feel like a "member"?

COMMUNITY!

For example, think about a gym membership.

- CrossFit
- Crunch Fitness
- Iron Tribe
- Orange Theory
- Gold's Gym
- LA Fitness
- The Zoo
- Planet Fitness
- Equinox Fitness Club

Every single one of these (and the many others not listed) have their own community. They have their own identity. They create members under their community.

I dare you to challenge a member of CrossFit, telling them why Orange Theory is better. Or vice versa. Those businesses create loyal members, a fiercely devoted community.

My friend, Dan Kennedy, says, "Build an iron fence around your herd to keep the poachers out." In context, he's talking about your members. Your members make up your herd. And in order for you to have longevity in your membership there must be an "iron fence." This means you must create a community where your herd will gather, desire to stay, and have their needs met.

SEVEN WAYS TO BUILD COMMUNITY – AN "IRON FENCE" AROUND YOUR MEMBERS

1. You can build a community around your member's similar wants, needs, and/or desires.

They're coming to your membership seeking to fill some void. They're looking to get something that your membership will provide. Take that collective desire and turn it into a community... A community where it is safe to have that desire. A community where people can admit they have that need. A community where people are comfortable knowing that they're no different from anyone else in the membership. They all want the same thing.

Make it known. Let them know it's okay. Celebrate it and repeat it over and over again for every new member.

2. You can build a community around your member's stage of life.

In my lifetime we've witnessed the rise of the 55+ Lifestyle Communities. I've also witnessed the rise of organizations targeted directly at Mothers of Preschoolers (MOPs). That's another stage of life.

The challenges of being retired, not being able to see your grandkids as much as you would like, and not knowing what to do with your time are very different from that of a mother of a preschooler.

And a mother of a preschooler will have very different needs than those of a mother with a teen. Even though both are parents, they are in a very different stage of life. One is just starting out in parenthood. The other is on the homestretch. Empty nest could even be on the horizon.

Gather these groups together and sure, they'll find some commonalities.

Separate them, putting them in their own stage of life though, and they'll have even greater community.

Like attracts like. It's a natural law. It's at work within your membership. Leverage the law to create community and greater value in your membership and your members will want to stay.

3. You can build a community around your member's profession.

You create this community by helping members through the challenges of their profession. You help them build the comradery that their profession provides: the stress, victories, talent, obstacles, tools, education, demands, and more.

If you put a group of lawyers in a room and add to it a group of periodontists, they're going to be very different from one another.

One group will know the proper procedures to file a harassment law suit. The other will know how to perform a gingival graft. (I know this because I've created memberships for both professions.)

A special note to Professional Associations. Too many times the association is solely focused on the profession. You would serve your members better by also focusing on the community that your association is able to provide.

4. You can build a community around your member's gender.

This is one of the longest running ways to build community. In many ways, it's obvious. Men and women see life in different ways.

Even though this may be obvious, it's often not leveraged enough. Maybe it's the cultural "Gender War" where people are making it harder to be vocal about the difference of the two genders.

But when you realize that your membership may be best able to help one gender over another, then you have a greater ability to create community.

I've worked with both... memberships that were best able to help women and memberships that were best able to help men. They didn't forsake the other gender. They were truthful about who they were best able to help, and they built a community around it. And yes, that community was accepting of the other, but you just might feel out of place.

Admittedly, this isn't for every membership and association. The goal is to know that if you're best able to help one gender over the other, then why not build a community around it. If you're not intentional about doing so, it will still happen. You'll just fail to be strategic about it when you leverage for community among your members.

5. You can build a community around your member's beliefs.

For some memberships, this is core to who they are as humans. For example, the church is a membership organization. The church has a specific belief system and to identify as a member you must adhere to that belief system.

It doesn't mean you can't attend. It doesn't mean that you can't participate. But if you really want to identify with that community, then you must accept that belief system as your own.

There are many others. I have a number of clients from the "real estate investing community." The "real estate investing community" isn't my term, that I made up. It's a term that has become widely accepted as being a community of people who believe you can create wealth by investing in real estate.

Your membership most likely has a belief that "doing it our way is the right way." This belief leads people to believe that what you provide as a membership is superior to what others provide.

Why not leverage that belief and create a community around it?

One of the memberships I helped build is a community for "Renegade Pastors." We wanted pastors to believe that it is possible to "abandon average in life and ministry."

That can be true of many memberships. You want your people to be a "Renegade" and to "abandon average."

When you build a community like that it also creates a desire to be part of it. We had people joining our membership just so they could call themselves a "Renegade."

6. You can build a community around your member's socio-economic status.

There's an affinity among the different socio-economic classes. It's not just true for one, it's true for all of them. They face different challenges. They have different tastes. They may have different desires. Where they live is different. Where they work or the position within their workplace is different.

Your membership may be best suited to cater toward one socio-economic class over the other. If this is true, you can leverage it to create a community.

Sometimes it's a literal community. I was invited to speak at a national event for country clubs. There were clubs from Australia and Canada, but most were from the United States. Every single one of them needed to provide an affinity among their members.

They're providing a haven away from those who are not in a similar socio-economic bracket. A place where no matter your religion, race or gender, they have an affinity community based on their income.

I've worked with other memberships to create this status based on a member's business revenue – those who have revenue of less than $250k, $250k-$500k, $500k-$1M, $1M-$5M and $5M+. Those businesses have different challenges at each level of revenue.

When you create this community, you're building an affinity among your members. That affinity relationship is one that makes them want to stay and refer other members to join in.

7. You can build a community around your member's hobbies and sports.

Even if your membership is not built around a particular hobby, you can leverage hobbies and sports to build greater community.

Many businesses are now using sports and different activities for "team building." Membership businesses are catching on.

Some of my private clients who host conferences and seminars are adding these team building activities into their events. They often revolve around sports or hobbies that their members already have an interest in.

Sports and hobbies not only create a team building experience, but they also create competition. People love to compete, but even more, they love to win. Who doesn't? Putting your members into teams and creating a competition where they compete against one another enables them to enjoy a sense of community within your membership that cannot be replicated in any other way.

These are just seven of the ways that you can create community within your membership. There are more. The key is to utilize as many as possible to create your community. You don't have to use all of them at all times. That would be too overwhelming for your members.

However, there's a time and place for each of these community builders to be used and leveraged to foster greater community in your membership.

When you do this, you keep your members from leaving. The desire to go elsewhere decreases and the desire to stay engaged and a part of the community increases. This will increase your overall retention of your membership.

"In just the first 30 minutes of going through Scott's program, we were able to multiply our membership revenue path more than 300%!!"

—Kim Walsh Phillips, Powerful Professionals

"It's not an exaggeration to say that this network wouldn't exist without Scott Whitaker. After hearing me say for years that I wanted to build a network for renegade pastors, he finally cornered me (literally) in a hotel lobby in Southern California and told me it was time to put action behind my words (at least that's what I heard him say; I'm sure he was more tactful). Two months later, The Renegade Pastors Network was born. Thank you, Scott!"

—Nelson Searcy
Founder, The Renegade Pastors Network
Church Leader Insights

THE 5-C MODEL OF MEMBERSHIP MARKETING – GETTING AND KEEPING YOUR MEMBERS

Much has been written about how to market to acquire customers. Take a walk through your local bookstore (if you can still find one) or browse through Amazon and you'll see all sorts of books on marketing. However, very little has been written on "membership marketing."

That's because people fail to realize that marketing for membership businesses is different. We have to not only market to GET members, we must do marketing to KEEP members.

In most membership businesses the marketing stops once the person becomes a member. I'm not talking about the marketing you're doing to invite people to become a member, I'm referring to the marketing that you must do to affirm the decision your member made to join.

The marketing that you do to keep members includes:

- Reminding them of their benefits.

- Reminding them that what they're receiving is for "members only."

- Reminding them that those outside of the membership don't have access to the same benefits.

- Reselling them on membership renewal. (This may be the one key that is keeping people from renewing their membership with you if you're not constantly reselling them on the membership.)

So how does this look for a membership? How do you market to GET and KEEP members?

There's a simple 5-C Model of Membership Marketing™ that will guide your marketing.

It looks like this. Your marketing should:

1. Move people from your CROWD to CONTINUITY

2. Move people from your CONTINUITY to COMMUNITY

3. Move people from your COMMUNITY to COMMITTED

4. Move people from your COMMITTED to CORE

#1: Moving people from your CROWD to CONTINUITY

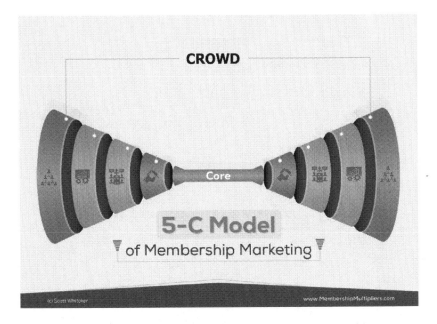

WHO IS IN YOUR CROWD?

These are the non-members that you're best able to help with your membership. If you're going to move these people out of the crowd, you need to know who these non-members are.

Call it an avatar, an ideal member, or prospect profile, but you need a good understanding of who your prospective member is so you can best target your marketing.

You can do this by asking:

- What does your prospective member like?
- What does this person dislike?

- What are their goals?

- Where does this person live?

- Where does this person work?

- Is this person married, single, or divorced (and does it matter?)

- Does this person have kids? (and does it matter?)

- What's their level of education?

- How much money does this person make?

- What does this person like to read?

- What conferences does this person attend?

- Where does this person get information?

- What other organizations might this person belong to?

- What are this person's pain points?

- Why would this person need your membership program?

- Does this person have the decision-making power to buy your membership program?

Once you answer these questions, you'll have a clear picture of who your prospective member is, and then you can go about moving them to your "continuity."

HOW DO YOU MOVE YOUR CROWD INTO YOUR CONTINUITY?

By "moving into your continuity," I mean how do you get them to sign up for your membership. The sign up to your membership is the transition moment from crowd to continuity.

The moment they sign up, they're no longer a part of the crowd. They're a member!

But how do you get them to sign up?

Most membership businesses build a sales page on their website and hope that people will just sign up. After all, it's online, so surely it will sell.

You have to make them an offer to join your membership. Most membership businesses think that their membership itself is the offer. It's not. Instead your membership has to be the solution to a need, want, or desire that your prospects have.

Once you have created an offer, you need to market it to your membership. I'll talk more about this in the "Accelerator: The Best All-Time (But Least Used) Method to Multiply Your Membership" section on page 81.

As you begin to market your membership, you need to structure a deadline. Most membership business leaders think they can't have a deadline. Why? Who said that was a rule for running a membership?

The truth is that most people don't do what they should, they do what's urgent. A deadline helps create urgency within the mind of your prospects and motivates them to join your membership (continuity).

#2 Moving people from your CONTINUITY to COMMUNITY

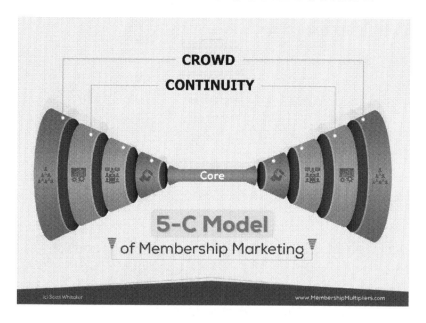

WHO IS IN YOUR CONTINUITY?

These are now your "new members." They're in the very beginning of experiencing the membership. They may not even fully see themselves as a member. They may say, "I signed up," but they've not taken ownership of their membership just yet.

That's why your marketing cannot stop. You now need to market to your new members to get them to use their membership.

Previously, you did marketing to get them to sign up for membership, now you're going to market to get them to use their membership.

In most membership businesses, the communications that go out to new members are the same that go out to existing members. But if you're going to funnel people from continuity to your community, you need to have specific communications that help them engage in their membership, resulting in them moving toward your community.

How Do You Move Your Continuity into Your Community?

1. New Member Event

Events make a great environment to gather new members and give them an overview, and/or introduce them to other new members. You can use this as an opportunity to build community with one another and your staff. Plus, you can invite some current members who may be social connectors to this event and help them build community with your new members as well.

This event can be hosted both in person or online. Tom Orent and Kim Walsh Phillips, two of my private clients, are having great success with these events. They possess members in broad geographical locations and so they host these events online. Their success is similar to that of those hosting such events in-person.

2. New Member Package

Sending your new members a "new member package" gives you a great opportunity to target your marketing to move them into your community. You can use this package to market the membership benefits, outline their "best next step" to take, encourage them to participate in their membership, provide member testimonies of current members, introduce key staff, and so much more.

If you have multiple levels of membership, you can also promote the next levels. Let your new members know there are options available to upgrade their membership and educate them on how to do so.

3. New Member Welcome Phone Call

This is a scripted phone call to personalize the membership. For most membership businesses, the sign-up takes place online. That can make it impersonal, leaving your new member feeling like it was more of a transaction.

Making a personal phone call, even if it's just a voicemail, will help your new member engage their membership, encouraging them to take action.

To make the most of the welcome phone call, use a "new member welcome call script." Have a script written out so that whoever is making the phone call knows exactly what to say and knows how to answer anticipated questions. There should be one script for when someone answers the phone and another for leaving a voicemail.

4. New Member Emails

Have you considered what your new members are receiving via email? When I ask that question, many times I discover that new members continue to receive email promotions inviting them to sign up. At the very least, they should be removed from your marketing to non-members.

Once you remove them from your marketing to non-members, why not market them the benefits of their membership instead? Why not send them an email letting them know how to use their membership, what they should do first, and what they should do after that?

You can create a new member email campaign that guides them into the community of their membership and gets them to engage with their membership.

5. New Member Orientation

An orientation is a great next step to move your members into community. "Orientation" suggests this is the best way to familiarize yourself with your membership.

People don't like the unfamiliar. It's out of their comfort zone. By creating a new member orientation, you are making the unfamiliar, familiar. You're getting them outside of their comfort zone and creating comfort. Build an intentional process to make your membership familiar.

6. New Member Tour

For those memberships that have a physical location or an online membership site, give your members a tour. Take them around your location and let them see the different areas of your location. This is great for country clubs, gyms, or any membership that requires people to go to a physical location to use their membership.

Online membership sites are a great modality to deliver membership benefits. However, even for the most tech savvy person, an online membership site can be confusing. Instead, create a video tour of your membership site and let them see what is located where, how to update their information, and where they should go to get the most out of their membership site.

These are just six ways to market your membership & move people from Continuity to Community.

Visit: www.AcceleratorBook.com

for sample emails, videos, and scripts that you can use in your membership.

#3 Moving people from your COMMUNITY to COMMITTED

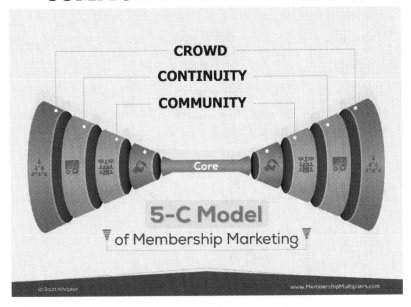

WHO IS IN YOUR **COMMUNITY?**

Your community is made up of members who have been engaging their membership in a continual manner. This is where most of your membership resides. They use their membership. They receive the value your membership program provides. They would identify themselves as a member.

However, if given a better opportunity they may go somewhere else. If a competitor makes them an offer or entices them, they might just cancel and never return. Plus, the membership is still low on their priority list and runs the risk of them just not using it.

The goal is to market to your community to get them to use their membership in both a consistent and predictable manner.

Who is showing up for your membership? Can you name them? More than likely you know to "anticipate their participation."

For most membership businesses this is left to chance. There's not an intentional process to move people from just using their membership to a place where you are able to anticipate their participation.

How Do You Move a Member from Your Community to Becoming a Committed Member?

1. Make communication two-way.

Encourage members to respond to your communications, reply to emails, and engage in conversation. When you see members responding to communication, you will begin to see their commitment to the membership increase.

These are members who are actually responding to communications. You know your communication isn't falling on deaf ears because your committed members are responding.

2. Create opportunities for a deeper relationship.

They identify with the membership, other members, and with the benefits they're receiving. Committed members identify with your membership program. It's part of their life.

I go into greater detail on relationships in The 2xR Retention Method™. But through your marketing you can encourage people to move forward in their membership in such a way that they begin to identify with the benefits, members, and even staff members.

3. Encourage members to give testimonies.

Testimonies are a great asset for any membership business. When someone gives a testimony of how your membership has benefitted them, they're not only telling their story, they're now creating a deeper obligation to continue with the membership.

A testimony endears a member to the membership and holds them accountable. "If I just said all of those things about how the membership benefited me, why would I quit now?"

4. You see them benefiting from their membership.

Your own observations of members benefitting from the membership can be an indicator of them having a greater commitment. You see them benefitting, you notice their improvements, these are all indicators of members moving toward a greater commitment.

The goal is to create marketing communications to encourage this movement toward greater commitment. I like to call it "Marketing for Commitment."

#4 Moving people from your COMMITTED to CORE

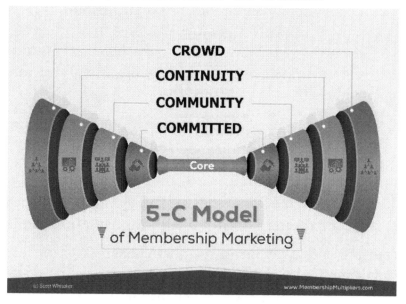

WHO IS **COMMITTED** TO THEIR MEMBERSHIP?

Your committed members are those from whom you can anticipate participation. You see and hear from them often. When you host an event, you know you can count on them to show up.

They're adjusting their priorities around the membership because it has increased in priority for them.

So how do you move people from just being committed to being in your core?

The best way to do this is to give core members responsibilities. When you assign members a responsibility you are then able to hold them accountable to that responsibility.

Responsibility

+ Accountability

+ Reward

= COMMITMENT

RESPONSIBILITY

What volunteer opportunities can you create within your membership? Some of the action steps that this book has generated for you, may prompt you to question, "Who is going to do this?" Why not look to your membership to help?

Consider these responsibilities as volunteer positions. Some responsibilities that are greater may require paid volunteers, but most responsibilities can be accomplished by unpaid volunteers. People want to be part of something greater than themselves. They want to give back, and your membership may be the best opportunity for them to do so.

Members who are committed want others to experience the benefits they have experienced. They want to tell others. They want to help others have the same great experience.

Responsibilities, great or small, will help your members move toward commitment.

ACCOUNTABILITY

If you're going to give responsibilities, you need to have accountability. Accountability is simply affirming, encouraging, and gently instructing volunteers in their responsibility.

People will rise to the occasion. But many will only do so if they're being held accountable.

A simple "check-in" with them to see how things are going will help. Ask them if there's anything they need to better fulfill their responsibility.

REWARD

There's no responsibility without accountability AND reward.

Who doesn't love to be rewarded? Everyone does! That which gets rewarded gets repeated.

The reward should be:

- Unexpected
- Given in a timely manner (as close to the responsibility as possible)
- In proportion to the responsibility
- Personal

However, different people like to be rewarded in different ways. This is true for staff and volunteers.

For some people the best reward may be:

- Words of encouragement
- Time (time with others, you, or staff)
- Gifts (in proportion to the responsibility)
- Recognition – this can be both private or public recognition

- Access – to tools, people, or resources

As you give people responsibilities, hold them accountable, and reward them, you'll increase their commitment to your membership. They'll be looked upon as the core of the membership. They become the member whom others look up to and aspire to model.

> "While working with Scott, I have been able to move new members to fully-engaged and strengthen client loyalty. The best part is that together we were able to create a solid system that my staff can implement so that each new member will know that their investment with us is one of the best decisions they have ever made. Thank you, Scott, for taking things and putting them into a simple process that will increase our revenue and more importantly our client loyalty."
>
> —Jennifer Sanchez, VP of Sales & Marketing,
> Beautique Medical Spa

You Can "Rescue People" from Canceling Your Membership

There's an old story about a terrible storm which came into town. Local officials sent out an emergency warning that the riverbanks would soon overflow and flood nearby homes. They ordered everyone in the town to evacuate immediately.

A faithful religious man heard the warning and decided to stay, saying to himself, "I will trust God and if I am in danger, then God will send a divine miracle to save me."

The neighbors came by his house and said to him, "We're leaving and there is room for you in our car, please come with us!" But the man declined. "I have faith that God will save me."

As the man stood on his porch watching the water rise up the steps, a man in a canoe paddled by and called to him, "Hurry and come into my canoe, the waters are rising quickly!" But the man again said, "No thanks, God will save me."

The floodwaters rose higher, now pouring water into his living room and the man had to retreat to the second floor.

A police motorboat came by and saw him at the window. "We will come up and rescue you!" they shouted. But the man refused, waving them off saying, "Use your time to save someone else! I have faith that God will save me!"

The flood waters rose higher and higher and the man had to climb up to his rooftop.

A helicopter spotted him and dropped a rope ladder. A rescue officer came down the ladder and pleaded with the man, "Grab my hand and I will pull you up!" But the man still refused, folding his arms tightly to his body. "No, thank you! God will save me!"

Shortly after, the house broke up and the floodwaters swept the man away and he drowned.

When the man stood before God and asked, "I put all of my faith in You. Why didn't You come to save me?" God answered, "I sent you a warning. I sent you a car. I sent you a canoe. I sent you a motorboat. I sent you a helicopter. What more were you looking for?"

What does this have to do with your members and them canceling their membership?

After growing a membership business to over 3,127 members, you will hear all sorts of reasons for canceling. Some I knew were true and some sure did sound like a made-up story just so the member could cancel.

However, after hearing hundreds of reasons for people canceling their membership, I've found that there are usually three general reasons people cancel.

PEOPLE CANCEL THEIR MEMBERSHIP BECAUSE:

1. They're in trouble

The trouble could present itself in several ways, but is most often dealing with the member's finances, marriage, job, or health. You've probably heard people say they need to cancel due to money or budget cuts, not to mention people losing a job, going through a divorce, or experiencing some sort of health crisis.

Psychologically, what they're experiencing is the membership being an added source of stress and the only way to decrease that stress is to cancel the membership altogether.

2. Going through transition

Transitions can come in the form of:

- Relocation
- Stage of life (just graduated, married, new child, retired)
- New job

When someone is transitioning, they're having to realign their priorities or their environment. In doing so, it may make it difficult for the membership to "fit" into this new arrangement of priorities.

3. Under some sort of tension

This tension can be felt through:

- Spouse or boss no longer wants them to have the membership
- Job stress

- Increased responsibilities

Go back to our story for a moment – if your member is going to cancel their membership for any of these reasons, why wouldn't you at least try to send him a car, canoe, motorboat, or a helicopter? Okay, maybe not literally one of those... by why not try to help your member through the trouble, transition, or tension.

If you really believe your membership can help people...

If you really want to change lives...

Then HOW DARE YOU let a member quit!

Is it possible that your membership could be the one thing that helps this person through the trouble, transition, or tension? If not the one thing, could it be one of many things that helps?

When I work with a private client, I always ask the question:

"How do you process a cancellation?"

I was having a VIP Day with a private client and I intentionally saved the question for lunch. I knew that the membership business was in trouble. And I knew this was a big issue.

During the meal, I just casually asked, "So, when someone cancels, how do you process the cancelation?"

Immediately, the person answered, "We just go into our database and mark them as canceled."

I replied by saying, "So when someone emails that they want to cancel their membership, you just process it?"

"Yes!" they replied.

I said, "How dare you?"

Needless, to say, the person stopped eating and looked up at me.

"If you really believe that your membership is going to help them have a better business, experience greater financial freedom, have better relationships, help them help more people – How dare you let them quit!"

At this point, I had my client's complete attention. The tension in the room was thick.

I just let it sit. I wanted this person to think about it for a moment. I picked up my sandwich and took a bite. Meanwhile, my client looked like he had seen a ghost.

Finally, he broke silence and asked, "Well, what should I do?"

Here are three rules I shared:

1. Recognize every member matters.

When someone requests to cancel, pause and recognize, "this member matters." Why do they matter? Because if too many members cancel, you won't have a membership. You won't have a job.

But they matter more than that, because they matter as a person. When a member cancels, you're no longer able to help them. You lose the ability to influence them and give them all the benefits that your membership is designed to give.

The impact of your membership decreases with every cancelation.

2. Never process a cancelation without an offer.

Make them an offer to stay. There are a number of offers that you can make to them:

- Half price for a month

- Half price for two months

- Free month of membership

- Free two months of membership

- Free resource or tool (especially one that will help them through their trouble, tension, or transition)

Sometimes, the situation may lend itself to you just asking, "How can I make membership possible for you as you go through this difficult time?"

Genuinely, what I like to tell people who cancel is, "The last thing I want to do is let you cancel. Especially, if there's a way that I can help." It's genuine. It shows that I care. It shows that I value members. If you can truthfully say it, it's worth adding to your conversation.

Even if they still cancel, they'll appreciate you more for it.

3. Always leave an open door for them to return.

Membership has a lifecycle. Just because a member cancels, it doesn't mean they won't return. So, why not leave an open door for them to come back?

I've seen memberships where, if you cancel, they basically say, "You're dead to me!"

I know of one such membership business, that if you cancel your membership, you're literally blacklisted and are not allowed to rejoin. Never! Your email is removed, you're wiped from the database and put on a list.

As I listened to this person boast about his cancelation process, he bragged about how he had someone who canceled and tried to join again. The customer paid a membership fee and everything. This person then bragged about how he'd refunded the new customer and said that person was not welcome as a member.

I understand that some memberships have a waiting list, application process, or other means that might prevent a member from immediately returning.

But if you can create an open door... if you can create an opportunity for when they get past their trouble, tension, or transition to return, then you will help perpetuate the membership lifecycle.

When you set out to "rescue" your members from canceling, you're showing that you have a genuine interest in their well-being.

As you do this, here are a few more suggestions:

- **Do not continue to bill them for their membership.** There are some memberships that are giving the rest of us a bad reputation. They make it difficult for people to cancel. You can make it easy for someone to cancel their membership and billing, just difficult to leave and no longer be a member.

- **Put them in a "reactivation campaign."** They were once sold on your membership. This can make it easier to sell them again on your membership. Those members who have canceled can be some of the easiest to get to sign up. Why not market to them and invite them to come back?

- **Always smile!** Let's face it. Someone canceling their membership can feel personal to you. But their decision isn't personal to you, so smile and let them know it's okay to come back.

When you do this, you send your member a life preserver to help rescue them from canceling and they'll actually thank you for it.

Think about that – when is the last time a member thanked you for not letting them cancel? I've seen it happen all the time. You can have it happen, too.

For more help rescuing members from quitting, visit:

www.AcceleratorBook.com

THE DIRTY LITTLE LIE: "IF WE JUST ADD MORE VALUE, WE'LL GET MORE MEMBERS"

There's a dirty little myth out there – "If we just add more value, we'll get more members."

Sometimes the lie is said out loud. Sometimes it's an internal belief.

However, it all starts with, "Why aren't we getting more members?"

Somehow, the question of "Why aren't we getting more members?" was more easily answered by just saying, "If we add more value, we'll get more members."

It's a lie!

And it can lead to your membership going bankrupt and building an unsustainable model.

Most memberships don't have a value problem, they have a problem with their structure. I've yet to work with a membership business that has a value proposition problem. Instead every single one of them has a problem with their structure. Their foundation isn't sustainable or best able to help their members.

How Can You Build a Sustainable Membership that Will Attract More Members?

There are three C's to structuring your membership business for greater value and effectiveness that will actually attract more members.

1. CATALOG

This is your catalog of services, goods, and/or content that you can provide your members. It's everything, absolutely everything you can give people as part of their membership. This makes up your catalog.

Periodically, it's good for every membership business to go through the evaluation of asking:

- What are we good at?

- What are we passionate about?

- How have we helped others achieve what we've achieved?

- What content do we already have that is already helping others?

- What goods, services, or content do others have that we can provide as part of our membership?

- If we had the time to add new goods, services, or content, what would we create?

When you gather all of this together, this becomes your catalog. Again, never have I had a client say, "We don't have much!"

2. CATEGORIES

What categories do your goods, services, or content fall into?

Imagine for a moment if you went to your favorite restaurant. Let's take it a step further. It's date night and you and your significant other are going to your favorite restaurant. You've been looking forward to it all week. There's going to be great food and great company.

You walk in and they've been anticipating your arrival. They escort you to the best table in the house and you take your seat. Right before the hostess leaves, she presents you with your menu and says, "We have a brand new menu. I'm sure you'll enjoy it."

She walks away and you open your menu and... it really is different!

You were expecting to start with an appetizer but now you can't find them. You know the restaurant serves appetizers, but you don't see them listed anywhere.

You glance across the table to your date and begin wondering if it's just your menu. Maybe it's a misprint. When you notice the look on your partner's face though, it's as puzzled as yours.

Without saying anything, you look for the entrees and hope for something that may be appealing. You can't find those either.

Finally, you look across the table, and you ask your date, "Is there something wrong with your menu? I don't understand mine. I can't tell which is an appetizer, or what's an entrée. I don't even see the desserts. All I see are a bunch of ingredients."

The entire menu is listed by ingredients! It wouldn't take long before you decided to go somewhere else with a menu that makes sense.

That's what categories can do for you. They categorize your catalog into "appetizers, entrees, and desserts." Okay, not literally those categories. The names are up to you. You can categorize your catalog in a number of ways. Here are some of the most common:

- **Beginner, Intermediate, Advanced**

Are there goods, services, and/or content that is best suited for a beginner? Intermediate member? Advanced member? Why not divide your catalog over the levels of your membership?

- **"Done with you" or "Done for you"**

This is a category that you either "do with your members" or it's "done for your members."

- **"Evergreen" or "Time-bound"**

Evergreen means that the goods, services, or content can be used at any time. There's no specific time of day or calendar date when it is best used.

Time-bound is the opposite. This means there is a specific time of day, or a date on the calendar when your goods, services, or content is best utilized.

Think of this like a "breakfast menu," "lunch menu," and dinner menu." And then you might also have a menu that is served "all day." The "all day" menu is evergreen while the others are time-bound.

- **Process-Oriented or Organic**

Some memberships are process-oriented. That means before you go to step three, you must complete steps one and two. They must be completed in a specific order.

Organic means that it doesn't matter in what order members utilize their membership content. They can do it as they choose and customize it on their own. It's not a step-by-step process.

3. CALENDAR

Once you have your catalog and categories, you'll then be able to organize your goods, services, and/or content onto a calendar.

Many membership businesses leave the membership to chance. There's no structure for how to deliver the membership.

Why is it important to calendar your membership program?

- It reduces your stress. Instead, you will now know what you're going to do and when.
- It reduces frustration for your staff. They have a clearer picture of what needs to be done and when.
- It provides greater clarity for your members. It helps build anticipation about what they're going to experience.

You'll be able to clearly choose when you're going to deliver your membership, how you're going to deliver it, and when you will deliver it.

When you set an intentional plan for delivering your membership, you'll better recognize the value of your membership and it will become clearer to your members as well.

This will ultimately help you acquire more members. When your prospects can see the "menu" and it will make sense (not just a bunch of listed ingredients) then they'll want to stick around for the dessert!

"Scott Whitaker is wicked smart when it comes to planning strategy and tactical execution of all aspects of membership programs. From member indoctrination to renewal to ascension to selling and pitching, you will gain huge value from working with Scott. His ideas when implemented will result in a gain of at least half a million dollars in coaching revenue for my company. Scott verified and clarified things that my team has been telling me for how to change and improve what we do, but it took Scott to help me see the wisdom of changing things up, so we can deliver much more value and make much more money long term from our members. Hire Scott today! You won't regret it."

—Kris Murray
Founder of Childcare-Marketing.com

THE 2xR RETENTION METHOD™ – RETENTION IS EASIER THAN YOU THINK

There are two ways to grow your membership business:

1. Get new members
2. Increase your retention

Of those two ways, the fastest and cheapest method to grow your membership is to increase your retention. Think about it. If you increase the retention rate, it will benefit across your entire membership.

Say you have 100 members this month. If your current retention rate month over month is 60%, that means next month, you'll have only 60 members (without adding any new members).

Now you'll have to go and get 40 new members (costing you money) just to replace those members who canceled. And that's just to break even. You didn't grow your membership at all, because if you're successful you'll still have just 100 members.

Let's say you continue to grow your membership at the same rate (40 new members every month) while now you also seek to increase your retention.

You go to work on your membership, without spending any money and you increase your retention to 70%. You're now keeping 10% more of your membership every month.

Your numbers will look like this:

- Members at the beginning of the months = 100

- 70% Retention rate = 70 members

- New members sign up (same as previously) = 40

- You now have 110 members.

- The following month you'll have 117.

- The next month, you'll have 121.

- The month after that, you'll have 125.

You get the picture. That growth is all created by retention rather than trying to increase your 40 new members month over month. However... I like to do both! But, increasing your retention is the fastest way to growth.

For your free retention calculator and new member calculator, visit:

www.AcceleratorBook.com

and see how small improvements can lead to big growth in your membership.

How Can You Increase Your Retention without Spending More Money?

It's called the 2xR Retention Method™.

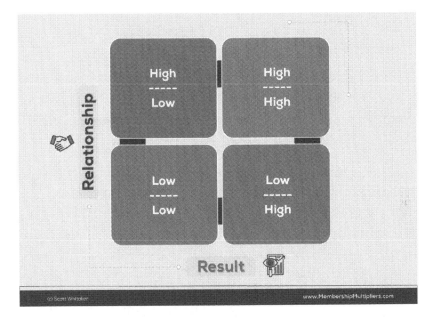

All of your members fall into one of these four quadrants. Let's clarify.

Relationships

- This can be a relationship with you, your staff, your members, or the affinity that your membership program provides.

Results

- This is the outcome your membership provides its members. It's the promise that you deliver on. It's what your members want out of their membership.

The 2xR Retention Method™ enables you to make those changes. Most of what is written on retention deals with tracking retention. This method however, gives you the tools you need to actually make changes to your retention and watch it increase.

1. Low Relationships / Low Results

When someone first joins your membership, they most likely fall into this category. They have a low number or quality of relationships and they have experienced no results from your membership.

You can't let members reside here. If they're not building relationships with others and they're not getting results from their membership, they're going to cancel. Why pay for something that's not getting what you want, desire, or need?

However, this isn't just where most new members start, this is also where many existing members may be. Existing members who decrease the use of their membership, stop using their benefits, and disengage from the community of your membership are also at risk of canceling.

2. Low Relationships / High Results

The member who has low relationships and high results says, "I'm getting a lot of value out of the membership, but I don't know anybody here."

Why does this matter?

All it takes is for one friend to come alongside your member and invite them to join a competing membership that they're part of. The threat you're facing is that your members will be lured away by others in their social sphere.

Quite often a new member will achieve results faster than they'll build relationships. That is why it's important to help your members craft those relationships at the beginning of their membership.

Your membership is probably best at results. That's why it takes an intentional focus to help members build relationships.

3. High Relationships / Low Results

The member who has high relationships and low results says, "I have great friends here, but I'm not getting any results from my membership. I'm not sure I want to pay to have friends."

This is the member who leaves because they see "greener pastures" somewhere else. They believe they can get greater results from a different membership program.

This is the threat you face from any competing membership businesses. All your competitors have to do is promote to your members the results that they can promise, and they'll entice your members away.

This is often a reason why members leave. They believe they can get better results somewhere else. A big reason this happens is that membership businesses don't do a great job of marketing to their members. They don't remind their members of the benefits they're receiving. For more on this, review the Accelerator: 5-C Model of Membership Marketing - Getting and Keeping Your Members on page 31.

4. High Relationships / High Results

The member who has high relationships and high results, has no reason to go anywhere else. They're getting what they want (results) and they have the relational backing to stay engaged in their membership.

When a competitor comes along, your member may try that membership program, but they won't stay because they continue to get the results they desire from your membership and they have the relationships, too.

When a friend comes along suggesting another membership opportunity that they're part of, your member will decline because they already have a community, and they're getting the results they desire.

Your members reside in one of these four quadrants. As your membership continues to grow, they will move to different quadrants. As some members cancel and leave, other members may lose some relational backing. After members get results, they may reach a point where they're no longer getting the results they once experienced. They can become stagnant.

There are other factors that can help you get your members results and relationships.

EVENTS

Events, seminars, and conferences are a great opportunity for you to get results for your members and simultaneously help build their relationships.

All of the membership businesses that I've worked with report having a greater retention rate due to the events that they provide their membership.

It's no coincidence in my opinion. It's because when you're at an event you have the opportunity to create new friendships and strengthen existing friendships just because of the environment that is created at the event.

Plus, the event's goal includes helping your members get the results they desire. You're giving them the tools, training, and/or resources that they would not necessarily have found apart from the event.

MEMBERSHIP CHALLENGES

Creating challenges and competition within your membership helps drive their relationships. They must work together to accomplish the challenge at hand. And at the same time they're working toward the end result that the challenge was created for.

No other experience can replace the relationships that are created during a challenge. When people have to come together to work and accomplish something that they could never do on their own, it results in a bond that is formed unlike any other.

SERVICE OPPORTUNITIES

Some membership businesses may benefit from creating service opportunities for their members. These service opportunities most likely will be some sort of community service projects... something that benefits others outside of the membership.

Many membership organizations may raise money for a particular cause, build a home through Habitat for Humanity, or sponsor a service project in their community. It's an opportunity for the members to engage in a project outside of the membership.

Similar to challenges, creating service projects enables members to achieve a goal and to do so in a manner that builds friendships. They are able to band together and do something that they would not necessarily do on their own.

Plus, they get the satisfaction of knowing they helped others who are in need.

Many membership businesses become so focused on tracking their retention that they fail to implement the steps needed to increase it. Yes! You should track your retention rate. But what are you going to do as a result of that tracking?

"Through Scott's 7-point plan and his proven experience, we were able to create a new level of membership that will significantly increase our monthly recurring revenue. Scott helped us identity underutilized membership assets we already had and capitalize on these, which went a long way to creating our new level of membership. He has a unique ability to develop programs, working backward from the desired outcome, and giving you the step-by-step execution plan!"

—Michael Rozbruch, CPA, Founder of Roz Strategies

THE SILENT "MEMBERSHIP KILLER" AND HOW TO STOP IT

There's a silent killer lurking in your membership business. No, it's not one of your members. It's not one of your staff members either (although there may be times where they want to, HA!). It's not your database, CRM, or marketing, either.

The silent killer... it's Member Overwhelm!

It creeps in, starting from the very beginning. Your prospect signs up and becomes a member. They think they have a good grasp on the membership but they're still learning (what all comes with the membership, what do they have access to, what do they not have access to).

But then, the current starts to build. More and more content comes their way. They try to use some of their membership only to get distracted by other opportunities the membership provides.

Before you know it, members are saying:

- "This is like drinking water from a fire hydrant."

- "There's so much, I'm just not sure what to do."

- "I keep getting all this stuff and my desk is piling up."

- "Seems like if I don't use everything, I'm not taking full advantage of my membership."

As the creator, you brush it off. You might even take a little pride in thinking, "Great! We offer a lot to our members."

Meanwhile, the countdown clock has started ticking and it won't be long before the overwhelm finally takes another victim and your member cancels.

It happens time and time again. But what can you do?

If we don't offer great value to our members then it may mean they'll cancel.

There's a simple way to ward off this silent killer.

MORE VALUE DOESN'T ALWAYS MEAN MORE MEMBERSHIP FEATURES

Many times less is more.

Would you rather help your members do a few things really well, or a lot of things very poorly? Most memberships want to help members do a few things really well. But in doing so, they offer a number of ways to accomplish it.

There's a way to provide great value to your members without overwhelming them.

Here are three simple questions that will guide you in this process, and help you utilize all the great work you've already been doing for your members.

1. What can you REPURPOSE?

You are probably offering way too much in your membership business. You're generously focused on trying to provide great content for your existing members – which you should be – but you're doing it at the disservice of attracting new members.

One of the barriers that is keeping you from getting more members into your membership program is that you're so focused on delivering what you said you were going to deliver, that you don't have time to focus on prospecting, let alone current membership retention.

As you begin to look at all the amazing content you've already created, ask yourself, "What is it that I can repurpose?"

Think about a video post, a blog, or an article that you wrote. Or think about some of the benefits that you're already providing. Now look inside that to find a couple of quotes you can pull out as social media posts. Then utilize these catchy memes to point people back to the article or a membership module where they can learn more.

If you blog, you can turn a series of blog posts into a book. With a little forethought, you can brainstorm a list of potential chapters for your book, then create two or three blog posts around each chapter's topic. Continue to do that, and soon you've not only written a book, but you've written a bunch of blog posts to go along with it... and pulled a massive number of quotes for social media to drive new traffic to every product you have to offer.

From those blog posts, you can also put together longer articles that can be re-published in print and online magazines within your industry. Consider aligning with organizations that reach your target market in a way you haven't yet been able to harness. Wouldn't it be amazing to capture new leads from an audience you didn't have to build yourself?

Also consider packaging marketing campaigns that you're doing in the B2B world – business to business – where your members would actually benefit from having a swipe file as a model, which they can use for themselves.

Again, this step is all about taking what you're already doing and repurposing it or repackaging it... putting it together in new ways. If you're already doing it, why not find multiple ways to use it? That's repurposing!

2. What can you RECYCLE?

There's an old proverb that "Repetition is the mother of learning." It's true! And "Recycling is a close cousin."

Think about a book or article you read last month or even last year. What can you remember from what you read? What topic was covered in chapter three? What's the next step you needed to take to maximize what you learned? Could you benefit from repetition of best practices to help you move forward?

Remember that your members, just like you, have to hear certain things multiple times before they are able to retain and achieve maximum benefits. While I'm not encouraging you to re-sell old content as a new product, I do want you to understand the power of reminding your members of valuable perennial lessons.

If you provide services, how many times does your member need to do something to create a habit? How many times do you need to get them into your gym for them to make it a habit? How many times do you need them to use your tools in order for them to become a novice, not even a pro... just a novice in their experience level?

It could also be that there are certain seasons of the year which lend themselves to your members being reminded of certain benefits. If you created a fall special for last year, why not re-use that same marketing promotion next fall? If you launched a Summer Bonus last June, it's time to dust it off and recycle it with no extra effort.

Examine each month of the year, different holidays, and different life/business events that affect your members. What messages could they benefit from hearing again? How soon do they need to receive this information again? When does this service need to be re-emphasized? When does this educational piece need to be re-presented?

That's how you recycle. Use what you're already doing for your members... the people who most need what you offer... to help remind them of the basics that so often fall out of sight when bombarded by a million daily messages.

3. What can you REFRAME?

Reframing is providing a different context to what you already provide. Think of it as applying a different media or a different modality to help members in various ways.

When reframing, you're giving old benefits a new look or a new feel. Think about how books often get updated, expanded, and rebranded. Perhaps the author has gone in and added a little bit, maybe taken away a little bit, and changed some of the stories, but the basic content inside that book is still the same. It's just been "updated and expanded."

If you were to look at what you did a year ago, months ago, two years ago, three years ago, and bring it forward – updating it, expanding it, making it fresher and better, more appealing – what would that look like? That's precisely what's meant by reframing. We're going to make it new all over again.

This is something you can do for your members. Some will have been with you for a length of time, but you will also have brand new prospects and new members who have never experienced this content before. You're sitting on a golden egg and not realizing it's ready to hatch.

Plus, you will almost certainly have existing members who "heard it the first time"... *but did nothing with it.*

You can also reframe your marketing. If you sent a marketing email to your membership, you probably think, "Well, I did that marketing campaign. I can't use it again." Just remember that a percentage of your email list may never have opened or engaged with that content at all. And a substantial portion of those who did will not remember the wording of an email you sent last January.

To reframe email content, update the subject line, change the introduction and closing a little bit, then retain the content of the email exactly the same as what you sent earlier. Your prospects and members need to be told again. We all need to be reminded.

This also works for the offers you've created. Don't believe you can't use them over and over again. Now, you might need to give them some time. Let it breathe. Remember to keep providing and demonstrating value! You don't want your prospects to believe all you're trying to do is constantly sell them.

In general though, you're creating too much, you're doing too much, and you're not allowing your members to fully soak in the most important aspects of what the membership already provides. Whenever we learn new things, it requires repetition and practice to not just understand the skills we're acquiring, but to internalize them and make the most profound life-altering transformation your membership set about to offer in the first place!

One of the more advanced tools that I encourage membership businesses to have is an **Engagement Tripwire.**

An Engagement Tripwire is an action that you want every member to take with the goal of getting them to use their membership.

When you think about your how you get members fully engaged, do you have a tripwire that moves them to take their first steps to use their membership?

What are the first 3-5 actions you want new members to take, especially those which will help them use their membership?

With each of these action steps that new members take, it should pull them further and further into your membership, increasing their engagement and utilization of "their membership."

Welcoming a new member is not enough!

You must move beyond welcoming a new member and actually guide them into their membership.

If you utilize an Engagement Tripwire, new members will:

- Assimilate more quickly
- Get a "quick win" in using their membership

- Feel more confident that joining your membership was indeed the right decision

- Will know immediately what they should do upon becoming a member

- Feel more like a member

Engagement tripwires should also be used in increasing your retention.

What are two or three actions that will increase engagement so members stay in your program longer?

The first step to utilizing engagement tripwires to increase retention is to look for the drop-off points where people are quitting their membership.

Usually, the drop-off points come because of:

1. **Time:** They've been a member for a specific period of time and are unengaged.

2. **Utilization:** They've not been using their membership.

3. **Payment:** They notice a payment.

4. **Value comparison:** They begin to question the value of the membership compared to their time, investment, your competitor, etc.

5. **Priorities:** They have so much going on they question whether or not they're going to make time for their membership.

6. **Overwhelm:** They get too much with their membership and feel like they're not utilizing it enough because they're not using everything that the membership makes available to them.

The second step to utilizing engagement tripwires to increase your retention is to establish two to three actions for each of those drop-off points.

The goal of these actions is to combat the drop-off point and re-engage your members. It's to pull them away from the drop-off and into your membership.

Remember that silent killer, "membership overwhelm"? Well, we just removed it from your membership.

Your members will now move from feeling overwhelmed to fully engaged and begin to get the most out of their membership.

"In just 24 hours our membership conversions went from 14% to 71% with one simple tweak that Scott made."

—Bill Heid, President, Heirloom Audio

THE BEST ALL-TIME (BUT LEAST USED) METHOD TO MULTIPLY YOUR MEMBERSHIP

Most membership businesses don't really believe me that they can actually MULTIPLY their membership.

"It's simply not possible!" is what they say.

I'm about to challenge the way you look at your membership business. In doing so, I want you to set aside the misconception that it's only possible to add members, and instead believe that you can MULTIPLY your membership.

Not too long ago, I was able to take my youngest daughter, Emily, to the Dead Sea. The Dead Sea is the lowest elevation on land at 1,237 feet below sea level. As we were riding down the world's lowest road, Highway 90, our ears began to pop as if we were in a plane.

What's interesting about the Dead Sea is that there is only one river which feeds into it. That would be the Jordan River. The Jordan River flows from the Sea of Galilee south to the Dead Sea.

You probably already know that what makes the Dead Sea a big tourist attraction is the fact that you can easily float.

The Dead Sea is actually a hypersaline, landlocked lake. The concentration of sodium chloride and other mineral salts is what causes you to float.

It's a great experience to float in the Dead Sea. Literally, you cannot go under the water, no matter how hard you try.

Most membership businesses are like the Dead Sea. They provide a great experience, a great place to hang out with others. Some even provide great memories, just like the memories Emily and I now share.

However, there's a more unfortunate way that membership businesses are like the Dead Sea. It's the fact that they only have one river feeding them.

> *Most membership businesses only*
> *have one way for people to sign up*
> *for membership.*

There's only one way into the membership (adding).

You may be saying, "But wait. People can sign up online, via email, phone, or even by application. I have multiple ways for people to sign up."

But those are only modalities. Those are the means by which people sign up for membership. I'm not referring to the modalities by which people sign up. I'm referring to the marketing methods by which you get people to sign up for your membership.

Most membership businesses only have one marketing method into membership. It's not emails (that's a modality), it's the invite (that's a method).

The single best way I've seen to move someone to membership is to offer a "Trial Membership."

A trial membership is an opportunity for your prospects to take a test-drive of the membership, before they make a full commitment to the membership.

A Trial Membership is:

- A "limited opportunity" to get the full experience of membership. They become full members (not partial) and experience what every other member is able to experience.

- NOT a trick used to get people's payment information so that you can keep on billing them.

- Able to be used in all different niches and types of membership businesses. I've yet to see a membership business not be able to successfully use a trial membership.

- Sometimes governed by state and federal laws and credit card processors.

No doubt that at some time you've probably experienced a trial membership. The problem that most membership businesses face is they don't know how to give prospects a trial membership.

There are three major components of a trial membership.

THE 3X FORMULA FOR TRIPLING YOUR MEMBERSHIP

1. Length of OPPORTUNITY

This is the amount of time that a new member will have for their trial membership. The trial can last seven days, 14 days, 30 days, 60 days, or even 90 days.

During this length of time, you're working to fully assimilate your new members into their membership. To move them from saying, "I signed up for..." to saying, "I'm a member of..."

This is your opportunity to give them the best experience possible so that they WANT to stay a member.

2. Type of OFFER

This is the initial offer that is being made to receive the trial membership. Some can include a dollar trial, free trial, just pay [insert amount], free trial with event registration, buy [product or service] and get a trial membership free, etc.

The type of offer is what you bundle with your membership to provide both the offer and the trial membership.

For every product or service you offer, you're able to bundle that with membership and create a trial membership.

They get to keep the offer even if they choose to cancel the membership later on. They're buying the offer and getting the membership as a test-drive.

If you don't have a product or service to offer, you can offer your membership at a discounted rate as part of the trial membership.

For example, "Get your first month half off!" The length of opportunity is the first month and the type of offer is the membership itself.

3. Sign-up OPTIONS

There are two types of options. These are:

- Forced Continuity
- Optional Continuity

Forced Continuity means that the only way people can take advantage of your offer is by buying it with the trial membership.

It is forced upon them. They cannot remove it from their shopping cart. The only way to get the discount or offer is to take it with the membership.

When using this option, you may see a decrease in the number of people who sign up, but every person will have the membership. The recurring revenue from the membership typically makes up the difference in the decreased number of buyers.

Optional Continuity means that a person can remove it from their shopping cart or from their purchase and just get the offer without membership attached.

For example, if you're offering a product at half-off with a two-month trial membership with optional continuity, then all they need to do is remove the two-month trial membership and they will still get the product at half-off.

When using optional continuity, you may see an increase in the number of people who buy, but not every person will have the membership. There will be a decrease in the recurring revenue and possibly an increase in one-time sales.

Some have attempted to abuse the trial membership and actually trick people into membership and make it hard for people to cancel their membership. There's no room for that in our business.

I'm not a lawyer, nor do I claim to have knowledge of all the laws governing this process. Heck! Lawyers make and change laws faster than many of us can keep up with. But I do know that it is possible, and it is simple so long as you act in good faith. The laws are there to protect us good guys and go after the deceptive ones. Just don't deceive people and you should be fine (this is my non-legal advice).

When done correctly, the trial membership gives your prospects the best opportunity to try out your membership and enables their experience with your membership to reinforce their decision to stay as a member.

Have Multiple Trial Memberships!

Go back to the Dead Sea for a moment. Remember how it only has the Jordan River providing a source for its water? That's like most membership businesses.

There's only one offer being made to come into membership.

But when you use *"The 3X Formula for Tripling Your Membership"* you will MULTIPLY your membership.

Instead of having one offer...

Instead of having one trial membership...

Why not offer multiple trial memberships, feeding your entire membership businesses!

"The 3X Formula for Tripling Your Membership" enables you to choose from over 100 different trial memberships.

Here's an example:

Opportunity	Offer	Options
7 Days	$1 Trial Offer	Forced Continuity
14 Days	Free Trial Plus Purchase	Optional Continuity
30 Days	Free Trial, Free Product, Just Pay Shipping	
60 Days	First Two Months for Just $X	
90 Days	Free Trial with Event Registration	

And that's with just one product or service. For example, if you have three different products, you could have over 300 different trial memberships.

If each of those trial memberships, brought in just one member, you would have 300 new members! And that's if you only offered that trial promotion one time.

I want you to offer multiple trial memberships, over and over again. This is the best way to double and even triple your membership... again and again!

To learn more about "The 3X Formula for Tripling Your Membership" and double or even triple your membership, visit:

www.AcceleratorBook.com

"Since working with Scott and following his clear and excellent guidance, I have increased my income by 50% per month. He has also given me a better understanding of how to provide better service and increase the engagement of my members, and I'm seeing longer retention rates."

—Jeannette Koczela, Founder/President
Int'l Association of Professional Life Coaches®

Accelerator #9

YOU HAVE A BIG VOICE BUT YOUR MEMBERS DON'T HEAR IT

What do you want your members to believe? Wow! That sounds like a deep question, doesn't it?

True story, if I don't finish this book on time, my good friend and private client, Mike Agugliaro gets the keys to my BMW Z-4 convertible.

Mike is the Founder of CEO Warrior. He is leading a movement to change the lives and businesses of service business owners around the world.

I've been intrigued by what Mike is doing with men and women in the service business industry (think plumbers, HVAC, electricians, etc.) since having the first opportunity to consult with him on membership.

We were talking about his membership business and I shared with him my desire to write a book. That's when he turned on the heat.

I won't go into full details but somehow by the end of his questioning, I committed to write this book, get it done by a set deadline, and if it wasn't, I would give him the keys to my BMW Z-4 hard-top convertible.

Mike has a very strong set of BELIEFs for his members. On the next page, I share with you his "Warrior Creed." As you read through it, you'll get a better picture of how Mike challenged me to write this book and is using my car as leverage to get it done.

This is a great example of a set of beliefs in a niche (plumbers, electricians, HVAC, etc.) that you would normally think wouldn't be possible. If Mike Agugliaro can do it in his membership, so can you!

WARRIOR CREED

We are Warriors

We are Creators

We look to a brighter future for ourselves, our families, our teams, our customers, our fellow Warriors, and anyone else we meet.

We are Unstoppable

We accept that our current situation might not be ideal; however, we take responsibility for the way it is now, and we push through to the brighter future we envision.

We are Relentless

We fight against assumptions and limiting beliefs to leave our mark on the world and to create a better life for ourselves and those around us.

We are Leaders

We are always aware that others are watching (both inside the group and outside) and we conduct ourselves as such.

We are Servants

We serve generously because serving creates positive change in ourselves and in others.

We are Powerful

We access an inner power that drives us forward, creates positive change wherever we go, and leaves our mark on the world.

WE ARE WARRIOR STRONG

That's strong! That's a set of beliefs.

It makes me want to be part of his membership. And I can barely use a hammer, let alone lead a service business.

I've seen firsthand how his members WANT to be part of CEO Warrior membership just because of the beliefs that Mike impresses upon them with the Warrior Creed.

Now you get a better picture of how he's challenging me to finish this book or otherwise give him the keys to my car. (Update: this book was completed, published, and in Mike's hand well before the deadline. I get to keep my "mid-life crisis mobile." HA!)

And he's not alone!

Kim Walsh Phillips is another private client and Founder of Powerful Professionals whose membership has a set of beliefs as well.

Kim leads business owners from all different sectors and professions. Some are brick and mortar, some of them are online, some of them are product based, and others are coaches.

And yet, she has a very clear set of beliefs for these "Powerful Professionals."

This is a great example of a set of beliefs that spans beyond one specific niche, affinity group, and/or type of business.

POWERFUL PROFESSIONALS:

- **Don't make excuses, they make things happen.**

- **Are in control of their business.**

- **They are not victims.** If something needs to change, they don't dream it would be different, THEY MAKE IT DIFFERENT.

- **Know they were not created to fail.** They were created to THRIVE, and success is the greatest response to those who told them they can't.

- **Don't get even, they GET PAID.**

- **Choose to surround themselves with those who INSPIRE, ENCOURAGE, and EMPOWER.**

- **Recognize there is an abundance of business to be had.**

- **Choose who to work with instead of others choosing to work with them, and they joyfully say, "NO" to cheap jerk-faces.**

- **Are not distracted by the latest shiny object.** They are focused on proven strategies that fit in their sweet spot of gifts and talents.

- **Know that their passions are not an accident. They are their GOD-GIVEN SUPERPOWERS.**

- **Do not waste a dollar out of their pocket, minute of their time, or ounce of their talent.** They can't invest fast enough in the tools they need to get them to where they want to go.

- **Do not compromise on things most important to them.** They are flexible in their "how" but never flexible in their "why." Family and faith are not a distraction but a driving force.

- **Know that success doesn't always happen on the first try, or second or even the third.** But success is inevitable to those who keep trying. They don't give up when things get hard. THEY PUSH HARDER.

Powerful Professionals don't wish for change...

THEY ARE THE CHANGE!

As your read over Kim's set of beliefs for her members, you get a better idea of how she's able to attract businesses from all different industries and niches to her seven-figure membership business.

How about this one? Along with my friend, Nelson Searcy, Founder of Church Leader Insights, we started the Renegade Pastors Network.

At the time, I was serving as President of Church Leader Insights and knew of Nelson's desire to launch a new membership program called, "The Renegade Pastors Network."

At the core of the membership was a driving set of beliefs that Nelson had solidified. I had heard him speak for years about his desire for the membership program.

I finally convinced him that we should launch the membership, and within three weeks we had over 100 members.

How could we get so many members, so quickly? One of the drivers was the "Seven Commitments of a Renegade Pastor." This set of beliefs is core to the membership.

This is a great example of a set of beliefs that is very specific to a niche and specific group of people.

THE SEVEN COMMITMENTS OF A RENEGADE PASTOR

1. Follow your Lord

Doing the work of God without destroying God's work in you.

2. Love Your Family

Refusing to sacrifice your family on the altar of ministry.

3. Fulfill Your Calling

Becoming All God Has Called You to Be

4. Manage Your Time

Taking Control of Your Most Limited Commodity

5. Shepherd Your Flock

Demystifying Your Job Description

6. Maximize Your Church

Structuring Your Church for Maximum Impact

7. Expand God's Kingdom

Embracing Your Place Within the Bigger Picture

You now have three different membership businesses, with three different (but similar) sets of beliefs for their membership.

BUT WHY HAVE A SET OF BELIEFS IN YOUR MEMBERSHIP?

- Rallies your members around a unified purpose.

- Motivates your members to fulfill the goals of your membership.

- Unites your members. Brings out the commonalities they all share.

- Keeps your competitors away.

Let's unpack each of these.

Having a set of beliefs rallies your members around a unified purpose.

There's a Proverb: "Where there is no vision, the people will perish." When you have a membership business, you have a gathering of people.

But, it's more than that. Your members are looking for a desired outcome from their membership.

Having a set of beliefs, gives them a unified purpose. And when you give a group of people a unified purpose it helps generate community.

Motivates your members to fulfill the goals of your membership.

Having a set of beliefs will better help you fulfill the goals that your membership has set out to achieve.

Go back and read Mike's, Kim's and Nelson's beliefs again. All of these beliefs are about helping their members to fulfill the goals that their respective memberships provide.

The beliefs give members a greater understanding of the outcome that the membership seeks to provide.

Members have a clearer picture of what they can expect from the membership, and so everyone in the membership is on the same page.

Unites your members. Brings out the commonalities they all share.

You can take a group of people from all different backgrounds, races, creeds, ethnicities, genders, professions and give them a set of beliefs that they can all rally behind and you'll bring out the commonalities that exist in that group.

The beliefs of the membership become the beliefs of the members. Again, causing greater community.

Keeps your competitors away.

However, it's not all about community. It's also about keeping your competitors away.

Your competitors can potentially duplicate the outcome that your membership provides. They can duplicate the services, the products, resources, and some will even flat out rip you off and copy what you're doing.

But what they can't duplicate, what they can't copy, is the set of beliefs that drives your membership.

It's your beliefs...

It's your purpose...

It's your passion...

It's your voice...

...And your members need to hear it from you!

Your members need to know from your membership business what is the desired outcome. And these beliefs will help paint that picture and give you a bigger voice.

"Following our chat in Phoenix, I decided to put on one of these small two-day workshops that we spoke about, with the idea of paying $97 upfront and $397/trial membership. And in just over two weeks we managed to sign up 30 new members from the workshop. So, thanks so much for the idea, dude. I really do appreciate you."

—Oliver Billson, Founder
Oliver Billson Marketing

"Our membership retention has done better because of your input and expertise!"

—Roslyn Rozbruch, President
Tax & Business Solutions Academy

L.E.A.D. YOUR MEMBERSHIP TO MULTIPLY

Here's a powerful question for you to consider:

What one thing could you do over the next six months to DOUBLE or even TRIPLE your membership?

The first thing you need to do is believe that it is possible. Again, you must believe that something can be, before it will become.

But believing is not enough. You can't just sit back and expect something to happen just because you believe it will happen. I'm all for having faith, but faith requires action.

So, assuming you believe it's possible to double and even triple your membership in the next six months, why haven't you done that? What's one thing you can do?

First, let me say, *it's not your fault!*

No one is teaching membership businesses how to grow, let alone double or even triple.

The authors, consultants, marketers, and thought leaders out there who are telling others how to run a membership business, aren't running a membership business of their own.

Why is that?

How can you teach others if you're not in the trenches yourself and leading your own membership business?

For the record, I lead three membership levels in my own business. Even as a Pastor, I was always a big believer of *"Practice what you preach!"*

Next time you look for a membership consultant, ask them this one question:

"Do YOU have a membership business?"

On top of that, most membership businesses are trying to use principles intended for customer-based businesses. Sure, there is some overlap, but membership businesses are different.

We have members to care for, provide for, and lead. We have numbers and figures like MRR (monthly recurring revenue), churn, retention, and reactivations that are not part of the customer-based model of business.

I'm sick and tired of seeing membership businesses use tools and tactics that are not designed for membership. And as a result, their membership business is declining, hurting, and failing their members.

To combat this, I want to give you a little acrostic that I encourage my members to use to grow their membership business.

The one thing you can do is L.E.A.D. your membership business to double or even triple.

L – Learn

E – Evaluate

A – Apply

D – Develop

LEARN

Congratulations! By getting to this point in the book, you've already taken steps to learn more about what it takes to lead a membership business.

But what will you do going forward? How will you continue to learn? Here are some actions steps:

- Decide now what book you will read next.

- Decide now what seminar you will attend next.

- Decide now what membership coaching networks you will be part of.

BOOKS

Right now, as I'm writing this book, there are four other books on my desk which I'm currently reading. My Audible app (which I highly recommend) shows that I've listened to over 183 hours of books in just the past year.

If you're going to become the leader of a membership business, you must first become a leader.

All leaders are readers!

A friend of mine once shared some tips on how to read more that I'll pass along to you.

- **Don't be afraid to stop reading a book.** Sometimes the best thing you can do is stop reading a bad book. That way you can move on to a good book.

- **Get audio books.** Audio books are a favorite of mine. Especially when I travel. A good audio book with a good set of Bose headphones and I'm in my own little world.

- **Have a specific time of day.** Choose a time of day that works best for you. I like to read early in the morning.

- **Have a specific location.** Some prefer a quiet place, some prefer a crowded coffee shop. For some reason, I prefer a quiet coffee shop. Crowd or no crowd, put me in a corner chair with a Venti Raspberry Mocha Latte and I'm all set!

- **Have a reading plan.** Mix up your selection of books. If you're constantly reading the same topic, you're going to grow weary. Personally, I like to read books on marketing, business, personal growth and mindset, and spiritual growth. It's not to say I don't read other genres, but those are the books that fall within my intentional plan.

SEMINARS

It's unfortunate there aren't many seminars on the topic of membership. You may find some on subscription businesses though. And you should attend them. For some of them I've been a keynote speaker. At these events, you'll learn practical tools you can apply to your membership.

But make sure you attend every seminar, conference, and/or convention on the topic of membership (again, just be leery of any speakers who don't run their own membership business).

You should also attend as many seminars as possible **inside your niche or industry**. Keep up with the latest happenings and industry standards.

Attend seminars **outside your niche or industry**. When you do this, filter what you're learning through the lenses of membership. There's a great deal to be learned from other industries.

It's unfortunate, but you can't get a university degree in membership. So, if you want to go far, you've got to attend seminars.

COACHING NETWORKS

What coaching networks or masterminds do you belong to with the focus on growing your membership business?

Again, I practice what I preach. I'm currently a member of three coaching groups. They help me leverage my time, energy, and effort. They also give me an opportunity to learn from others.

In addition to being a member of those groups, I also lead my own coaching groups. (Big surprise, I know!)

The coaching groups I lead are for MEMBERSHIP BUSINESSES ONLY! If you don't have a membership business, or aren't seeking to start one, then you can't join. I won't let you.

If you're interested in learning more about how you can become a member of one of my coaching groups, go to www.AcceleratorBook.com.

EVALUATE

Julius Caesar once said, "Experience is the best teacher."

Well, Julius Caesar was wrong!

You can experience many things but that doesn't mean that you will learn from them.

---

*Evaluated experience is
the best teacher!*

Do you know how to train an elephant? Elephants are some of the strongest animals on our planet yet they can be held back by a simple rope. How is that?

When an elephant is young and small, trainers will tie a rope around its neck and attach that rope to a strong and secure pole. When the young elephant tries to walk away, naturally the rope and pole keep it from doing so.

The young elephant will push, pull, and do everything possible to escape but the rope and pole keep it from going anywhere.

The same thing happens over and over until eventually, when the rope is placed over their heads, the elephant no longer pulls or pushes to try to break free because it knows it can't. That is why in captivity you will see giant elephants standing passively with a rope tied around their necks that isn't attached to anything at all.

The elephant becomes so accustomed to being held back by the rope, that merely the rope itself keeps the animal in check.

Their previous experience tells them they can't break free, when they really can.

That's why you have to evaluate your experience. Even if you've experienced it before.

Apply this principle to your membership business. For example, when you do a "trial membership" and it doesn't work, you can't just say: "I tried that already and it didn't work."

No, *it's not that it doesn't work, it's the way that you did it that didn't work.*

Evaluate it. What can you learn from experience?

- Was it the wrong time?
- Was it the wrong offer?
- Was it the wrong message?
- Was it the wrong audience?
- Was it the wrong context?
- Was it the wrong way to communicate?
- Was it in the wrong place?
- What went right?
- What went wrong?
- What was missing?

- What was confusing?

This not only works for when things go wrong but also for when things go right.

It's my observation that a lack of evaluating when things go right, is the source for most people's problems.

It's not that the method doesn't work... it's that the way it was implemented didn't work!

Think about it, something goes great and we go on to celebrate. We totally skip over evaluating what made it great.

When something goes wrong, we immediately look for the reason why it went wrong.

If you want to run a successful membership business, you can't rely on experience alone. You must rely on evaluated experience of both your victories and your losses.

APPLY

What are you applying in your membership business right now?

A good place to start is: what are you going to apply from reading this book?

Have you gone to www.AcceleratorBook.com and picked up your free tools and resources?

Have you considered becoming a member of my membership (a membership just for leaders of membership businesses)? Private client?

Dare I say that no one else can accelerate your membership faster than I can. Modest statement, HA!

Take out your calendar right now, and look at the next week of Monday through Friday. What is something you've learned here that you can say, "I need to apply this"?

Maybe it's the same thing every day. You just need to apply one small habit, and let it evolve, letting it come to fruition in your life so that it's no longer a force. It's no longer something you have to plan for.

One of the things I do every now and then, is go on a diet. I know I should eat healthy all the time, but I enjoy my "daddy daughter doughnut" days as often as I can.

But, every now and then I get to a point where it's time for me to go to work on my health. There are certain habits and routines that I'll change, and so I'll apply new disciplines. I'll apply both new disciplines and new routines.

It's the same way in exercising your membership business. If you're going to grow, you have to have a daily, weekly, and monthly plan to make it happen.

What is one goal you can set out to accomplish over the next month? Write it down. Give it a deadline. Choose a reward for yourself. Tell someone and have them hold you accountable for it.

Then break down that goal into weekly focuses. What are four focus areas that will help you accomplish that goal? Choose one focus area for the next four weeks.

Turn that monthly goal into a weekly focus. Turn that weekly focus into daily actions. Reward yourself along the way and it won't be long before you're growing your membership like never before.

DEVELOP

What are you developing right now?

Maybe, an even better question is, who are you developing right now?

There are three key areas of development that you should always be aware of and have an intentional plan to develop.

1. **Yourself**

2. **Those Around You**

3. **Your Business**

There's already a great deal written on goal setting. My point isn't to elaborate or even repeat what you may have already heard, but rather to challenge you.

I call it **The 100 Goal Challenge**. It's a challenge someone once gave me and one that I've repeated over the years and used with my members and private clients.

It's simple – write out 100 goals. While it may sound simple, you will probably find the process a little more daunting. Somewhere around goal 37 you'll likely find yourself thinking, "I still need to write 63 more goals."

Ralph Waldo Emerson suggested, "The mind, once stretched by a new idea, never returns to its original dimensions."

This process is about stretching you more so than it is about settin out to achieve all 100 goals.

However, you'll be surprised at how many of those goals you can actually accomplish just by having written them and having set your mind to intentionally accomplish them.

What goals can you set for yourself? For those around you? And for your business?

What is your intentional plan to make those goals happen?

> *To learn more about how you can achieve your goals, both personally and for your membership business, visit:*
>
> www.AcceleratorBook.com

COMMITTING TO ACCELERATE YOUR MEMBERSHIP

The first time I tried to build a membership business, I didn't have a clue as to what to do.

I didn't have these accelerators that I've outlined in this book. I didn't have the numerous other accelerators that I've shared with my private clients and members. I didn't have the tools and templates that I'm sharing with you at www.AcceleratorBook.com.

I've already given you a number of ways to grow your membership business. And although I've given you a number of next steps, the quickest way to accelerate your membership is to visit www.AcceleratorBook.com and become a member.

I constantly tell my members that my business is on full display. You get to see and experience first-hand how to run a membership business by joining mine.

If I don't practice what I preach, my members will be the first to call me out on it. Unlike many other consultants and "gurus," I've got a true membership business. I'm not just preaching to others about what they should do, I'm doing it myself.

When I make a mistake, my members get to learn from it so they can avoid the pain and costly error in their own business.

And at the same time, they get to implement the proven methods in their business and have me by their side to help them get more members.

At this point, you really have two decisions:

1. **You can continue to go about your membership business through "trial and error."**

It's a valid method. It's a method that has unfortunately cost me the most money. I didn't have the benefit of learning from someone who is solely focused on helping me get more members and increase my recurring revenue.

I get it. It's a default circumstance for many people. Not to mention, you may have had your trust broken by others who promised you results but failed.

However, it's been my experience, and the experience of many of my members before coming to me, that the "trial and error" method will:

> **Cost you more time.** You may reach your goal, but you most likely won't do it in the time that you're capable of doing because you don't have a proven process.

> **Cost you more money.** Right now, you're losing out on lost members. You're losing by not being able to help them, and you're losing on the monthly recurring revenue. For every month that goes by, it's lost revenue.

2. **You can take my proven accelerators and implement them in your membership.**

From what I've discovered there has yet to be a membership or association that hasn't been able to get more members, or even double or triple their membership using what I share with my members.

These accelerators work!

You're invited to become a member of the only membership that exists just for membership businesses and associations.

Join the community and get real-time feedback on your membership business from people who are in the trenches, just like you!

Most have found that they recoup their investment with just a couple of new members joining their membership.

You get recurring revenue! The members I get you in the first month should more than pay for the membership. Not to mention the members you're going to continue to get in the months to follow.

So, let's make it happen! Let's accelerate your membership so that you can achieve all that your membership business was intended to accomplish.

I look forward to seeing you on the inside at: www.AcceleratorBook.com.

"Scott Whitaker is a membership master! He gave me two tips in under five minutes that helped double our monthly membership revenue. Double! No bull, it is twice what it was and climbing. Scott is battle tested and knows his stuff. Give him a peek at your business, but only if you want to grow."

—Todd Tramonte, Real Estate Coach

"Before I met Scott and Membership Multipliers, I'd struggled for years to grow my membership. I launched it in 2012 at a low price point, not sure what I was doing but doing it anyway, with the high hopes of having 100 students by the year end, and then keep growing it every year. After all these years of effort, we couldn't seem to grow beyond 30 members. After working with Scott, in just a few months I've made changes that include raising the dues and adding 2 more levels of membership. We just finished launching Early Bird & Founding Member Platinum levels and now have 30 Platinum members, 24 Gold members, and 6 Silver members for a grand total of 60 members! I wish I'd met Scott years ago. It would have made all the difference!"

—Val Heart, Founder
Learn How to Talk to Animals

DON'T FORGET...

Claim your FREE tools,
templates and book extras.

Visit:
www.AcceleratorBook.com

About the Author

Scott Whitaker is an expert at building membership programs that will double your income in 90 days or less. He's most notable for having built a membership business from 72 people to over 3,000 people per month.

Through coaching and consulting, Scott is dedicated to helping you grow your business and getting you to that next level of success, no matter where you are in the process right now. Scott also offers limited on-site consulting and offers three different levels of coaching to businesses.

Scott is the founder of Membership Multipliers where he coaches membership business owners on how to get more members, increase retention, and multiply their profits.

He is the author of "Triple Your Membership in 21 Days... and Do It Over and Over Again Toolkit" and "Four Offers You Need to Have to Keep People From Quitting."

Scott has led membership organizations in both non-profit and for-profit companies since 1997. He's noted for having built the largest for-profit coaching network for pastors of churches, growing from just 72 pastors a year to over 3,000 pastors a year.

Scott and his wife Kelly have been married for over 20 years and have two daughters. They're foodies and enjoy traveling.

LinkedIn: www.linkedin.com/in/scott-whitaker

Facebook: www.facebook.com/membershipmultipliers

Made in the
USA
Columbia, SC